Remembering
Richmond

Emily J. and John S. Salmon

TURNER
PUBLISHING COMPANY

The Bell Tower, photographed in 1969, is located in the southwestern corner of Capitol Square. It was completed in 1824 to serve as a guardhouse and signal tower for the Virginia Public Guard, a forerunner of today's Capitol Police. The bell was rung in 1861 when the U.S. gunboat *Pawnee* approached Richmond several miles downstream, and also in 1864 when U.S. Army Colonel Ulric Dahlgren led an ill-fated raid on the city. It still rings daily when the General Assembly is in session to summon the legislators to the Capitol. In recent years it served briefly as the office of the lieutenant governor. Today, the Virginia Tourism Corporation maintains a visitor center in the tower.

Remembering
Richmond

Turner Publishing Company
4507 Charlotte Avenue • Suite 100
Nashville, Tennessee 37209
(615) 255-2665

Remembering Richmond

www.turnerpublishing.com

Library of Congress Control Number: 2010923497

ISBN: 978-1-59652-627-3
ISBN-13: 978-1-68336-878-6 (pbk)

Printed in the United States of America

10 11 12 13 14 15 16—0 9 8 7 6 5 4 3 2 1

CONTENTS

William A. Pratt built Pratt's Castle, also known as Pratt's Folly, in 1853. Pratt, an English entrepreneur who settled in Richmond in 1845, constructed the house on Gamble's Hill above the Tredegar Iron Works. Appropriately enough, although no connection with the ironworks is known, the castle was constructed of wood sheathed in metal plates. Pratt's romantic residence and its commanding views were especially noteworthy, because most Richmond houses of the period were Greek Revival in style.

Acknowledgments

This volume, *Remembering Richmond,* is the result of the cooperation and efforts of many individuals and organizations. It is with great thanks that we acknowledge the valuable contribution of the following for their generous support:

Library of Congress

Library of Virginia

Emily J. and John S. Salmon

PREFACE

Richmond has thousands of historic photographs that reside in archives, both locally and nationally. This book began with the observation that, while those photographs are of great interest to many, they are not easily accessible. During a time when Richmond is looking ahead and evaluating its future course, many people are asking, How do we treat the past? These decisions affect every aspect of the city—architecture, public spaces, commerce, infrastructure—and these, in turn, affect the way that people live their lives. This book seeks to provide easy access to a valuable, objective look into the history of Richmond.

The power of photographs is that they are less subjective than words in their treatment of history. Although the photographer can make subjective decisions regarding subject matter and how to capture and present it, photographs seldom interpret the past to the extent textual histories can. For this reason, photography is uniquely positioned to offer an original, untainted look at the past, allowing the viewer to learn for himself what the world was like a century or more ago.

This project represents countless hours of review and research. The researchers and writers have reviewed thousands of photographs in numerous archives. We greatly appreciate the generous assistance of the individuals and organizations listed in the acknowledgments of this work, without whom this project could not have been completed.

The goal in publishing this work is to provide broader access to this set of extraordinary photographs that seek to inspire, provide perspective, and evoke insight that might assist people who are responsible for determining Richmond's future. In addition, the book seeks to preserve the past with adequate respect and reverence.

With the exception of touching up imperfections that have accrued with the passage of time and cropping where necessary, no changes have been made. The focus and clarity of many images are limited to the technology and the ability of the photographer at the time they were recorded.

The work is divided into eras. Beginning with some of the earliest known photographs of Richmond, the first section records the Civil War era and decade following. The second section spans the closing decades of the nineteenth century. Section Three covers a broad swath of time, from the beginning of the twentieth century to the end of the 1930s. Section Four moves from the World War II era into recent times.

In each of these sections we have made an effort to capture various aspects of life through our selection of photographs. People, commerce, transportation, infrastructure, religious institutions, and educational institutions have been included to provide a broad perspective.

We encourage readers to reflect as they go walking in Richmond, strolling through the city, its parks, and its neighborhoods. It is the publisher's hope that in utilizing this work, longtime residents will learn something new and that new residents will gain a perspective on where Richmond has been, so that each can contribute to its future.

—*Todd Bottorff, Publisher*

This telegraph-construction wagon train arrived in Richmond soon after U.S. Army forces occupied the city in April 1865. The exact location of this scene is uncertain. During the war, the transmission of messages by courier was supplemented by semaphore or wigwag using flags, as well as by the telegraph. The military telegraph corps closely followed the Union armies, stringing wire to link not only one military unit to another but also to link generals in the field with Washington.

War and Reconstruction

(1860s–1879)

The U.S. Sanitary Commission established its headquarters in this building on the southeastern corner of 9th and Broad streets in Richmond after the war. Created in 1861 by Northern women despite some government opposition, the commission hired physicians to examine camps and recommend improvements in hygiene, augmented rations with more-healthful foods, collected and distributed medical supplies, and gave relief to sick and needy soldiers.

Many thousands of escaped slaves, known as contrabands, fled to Union lines during the war. Some attached themselves to the army and served as laundresses, teamsters, or servants. Others enlisted, joining free black men in regiments of United States Colored Troops; by war's end, about 200,000 blacks had fought for the Union and freedom. Wherever the federal presence became permanent, contraband camps sprang up, such as this one located in the lowlands of eastern Richmond between Church Hill (upper right) and the James River. It was established after the federal occupation of the city in April 1865. The Virginia state capitol is visible in the distance on the left.

Castle Thunder, located on the north side of Cary Street between 18th and 19th streets, was a tobacco warehouse before Confederate authorities used it to confine political prisoners, Unionists, spies, and common murderers. Little is known for certain about it, other than its reputation for brutal guards and grim conditions.

Some of the piers that supported the Richmond and Petersburg Railroad bridge, burned by Confederate forces during the evacuation on April 2-3, 1865, still remain in the James River today. The building on the left in this view looking south was a paper mill also destroyed in the fire.

This image, from the vantage point of the Richmond and Petersburg Railroad bridge ruins captured in the preceding image, shows the Confederate Laboratory on Brown's Island (left), salvageable bricks from the Virginia Manufactory of Arms neatly stacked (foreground), and the Tredegar Iron Works (right). Tredegar, the largest ironworks in the South, produced most of the cannons used by the Confederate armies. Several of its buildings still stand and have been restored. This National Historic Landmark operates today as the American Civil War Center at Historic Tredegar, devoted to exhibiting the story of the war from Union, Confederate, and African American perspectives.

Union soldiers pose with a ruined locomotive at the Richmond and Petersburg Railroad depot, near the site where the photograph of the railroad piers was taken.

This image, taken in April 1865 facing west, shows at right the ruins of the Gallego Flour Mills, which succumbed to the evacuation fire. The stone 11th Street Bridge, arching over the James River and Kanawha Canal, remains standing today. At the time of the war, Richmond had the largest flour-milling establishments in the United States.

Several photographs exist that show the wreckage of the burned district at Governor and Cary streets shortly after the evacuation fire. One, taken in brilliant sunshine, is devoid of people. Another, in gloomy low light, captures a pair of women in mourning black. This picture shows men posing like tourists amid the ruins, which look ready to collapse.

Both the Virginia state capitol at left, designed by Thomas Jefferson and begun in 1785, and the U.S. customs house in the center, designed by Boston architect Ammi B. Young and completed in 1858, still stand. Each has experienced additions, but they have been sympathetic to the original architectural styles—Classical Revival and Tuscan Palazzo, respectively. During the war, the Confederate Congress sat in the capitol, while President Jefferson Davis and his cabinet had their offices in the customs house. The James River and Kanawha Canal turning basin in the foreground is no more; surface parking and modern buildings have replaced it. In the 1970s, construction workers there unearthed the remains of a canal boat like the ones shown here.

Photographed probably in May or June 1865, this image of the Virginia state capitol from the northwest affords a view of the seldom-depicted rear and side of the building. It shows the original steps, which were on the eastern side as well, but were removed in the 1906 remodeling that added hyphens and wings to each side.

The Virginia governor's mansion on the northeastern corner of Capitol Square, photographed in April 1865, is the oldest governor's residence in continuous occupation in the United States. Alexander Parris, a New England architect, designed it, and it was completed in 1813. During the war, the body of General Thomas J. "Stonewall" Jackson lay in state there. The mansion is a National Historic Landmark.

Henry Clay was born in Virginia, although he is better known as a senator and statesman from Kentucky, as well as an unsuccessful candidate for president in 1844. After his defeat, a group of Richmond women organized the Virginia Association of Ladies for Erecting a Statue to Henry Clay. They contracted with a sculptor in 1846, but it was not until 1860, on the eve of the war that tore apart Clay's beloved Union, that the statue arrived. It was set up in this pavilion on Capitol Square and dedicated on April 12, 1860. Some years later, the pavilion was dismantled and the statue moved inside the capitol building.

The John Brockenbrough House, completed in 1818 at 1201 East Clay Street, is better known as the White House of the Confederacy. Jefferson Davis and his family resided here from 1861 to 1865. On April 4, 1865, the day after the U.S. Army entered Richmond, President Abraham Lincoln paid the house a brief visit. For the next five years it was a military residence, and then became a school. The Confederate Memorial Literary Society acquired it in 1893. Today this National Historic Landmark, restored to its appearance during the Davis occupancy, is open to the public as part of the Museum and White House of the Confederacy.

Governor or 12th Street, shown here looking east from Capitol Street, is one of the oldest streets in Richmond, appearing on the earliest maps as a "country road." It still winds its way down the hill to the river, and Morson's Row, constructed for John Morson in 1853, still stands on Governor Street across from the governor's mansion. Morson lived in one of the Italianate houses and rented out the other two. State offices now occupy the buildings, which today look just as they did in this April 1865 photograph.

Photographed from Main Street looking north, the eastern end of the U.S. customs house and the southern facade of the Virginia state capitol are shown here in April 1865. The evacuation fire stopped spreading north at Capitol Square, but not before destroying the courthouse in the southeastern corner of the square along with many irreplaceable documents stored there.

The Old Stone House, located on Main Street near 19th Street, has been the subject of much legend and lore over the years. It is often referred to as Washington's Headquarters, although there is no evidence linking him to the site. A recent analysis of its structural timbers supports a construction date of about 1754, and the first documented reference to an owner is to Samuel Ege in 1783. It is Richmond's only surviving colonial dwelling. Since 1921 it has been part of a museum honoring Edgar Allan Poe, who spent his youth in Richmond but did not live in the house.

This view of Main Street looking east from about 25th Street shows an undamaged part of the city in April 1865. Aside from the wagons and a few people on the streets, who undoubtedly are discussing recent events, there appears to be little traffic. The long exposure times required for photographs during the period, however, would render invisible anyone who did not stand still for a few seconds.

The Gothic Revival cast-iron tomb of James Monroe, a National Historic Landmark, stands in Hollywood Cemetery and dates to 1858, when the president's remains were reburied there from his grave in New York City. He had died and was interred in New York in 1831; 1858 was the centennial of his birth. Albert Lybrock, an architect who settled in Richmond in 1852, designed the tomb, which resembles that of Henry VII in Westminster Abbey. A landmark from its inception, the tomb has been the subject of many photographs, including this one taken in 1865.

The view of the James River from this perspective is believed to have inspired William Byrd II, founder of Richmond in 1738, to name the new town for Richmond-on-the-Thames just west of London, where the river view is nearly identical. The buildings and wharves constitute Rocketts Landing, for many years the port of Richmond, located just downstream from the city. This image, taken after Union forces occupied the city in April 1865, shows the side-wheel steamboat *Monohansett* in the river beyond the two large buildings on the right.

Monumental Episcopal Church, designed by Robert Mills, was completed in 1814. It stands on East Broad Street between 12th and College streets on the site of the Richmond Theatre, which burned during a performance on December 26, 1811. Seventy-two people died, including Virginia governor George W. Smith. The church was built to commemorate the victims. Today it is a National Historic Landmark owned by the Historic Richmond Foundation, which has undertaken a long-term restoration of the building.

The cornerstone of the Confederate Soldiers' Monument in Hollywood Cemetery was laid on December 3, 1868, after two years of fund raising; the capstone was set in place on November 6, 1869. Three presidents are buried in the cemetery: U.S. presidents James Monroe and John Tyler, and C.S. president Jefferson Davis. Other Confederate luminaries interred there include generals J. E. B. Stuart and George Pickett. About 18,000 Confederate soldiers, many of whose names are unknown, rest there as well.

To any resident of Richmond from its earliest days until the end of the twentieth century, this was a familiar scene: the James River overflowing its banks to flood Shockoe Bottom and Main Street between 15th and 17th streets (in the distance). The Old Market Building is in the middle ground on the left in this view, taken facing east on October 1, 1870, when the waters reached 24 feet in depth. In 1995, a floodwall was completed to prevent such catastrophes; ironically, the river has not reached flood stage here from that time to the present day.

Located at 7th and Broad streets, the new Richmond Theatre replaced an earlier theater in 1863, when it might be argued that Richmonders needed entertainment more than they usually did. The building was demolished in 1896.

PEACE AND GROWTH

(1880–1899)

After the Civil War, the federal government cared for disabled, sick, and elderly Union veterans and their widows and orphans. The care of Confederate veterans, however, fell to Southern state governments and benevolent societies. A group of former Confederates founded the Robert E. Lee Camp Confederate Soldiers' Home in Richmond in 1883, and the state provided increasing amounts of funding over the years. The Home, located on the present site of the Virginia Museum of Fine Arts, was operated with military discipline. Here a Grand Army of the Republic post—Union veterans from Lynn, Massachusetts—is pictured on a July 5, 1887, visit to their former adversaries in a spirit of reconciliation.

This scene was taken from the roof of the Virginia state capitol about 1885, facing northwest. Most of the buildings shown, beginning with the church on the right, stood on Broad Street. They were primarily commercial establishments, and they represent Richmond's recovery from the war and its aftermath.

Before electric streetcars came to Richmond in 1888, horse-drawn cars moved along steel tracks through the city's streets. City council approved the first such line on May 29, 1860, and it operated on Main and Broad streets until the war suspended it. After hostilities ceased, the Richmond Railway Company resumed service. The company went into receivership in 1881. Shown here is a car and team at the Richmond and Manchester streetcar barn.

This car belonging to the Richmond Union Passenger Railway, which operated the electric streetcar system, was photographed in 1888 near Broad and 29th streets on Church Hill. Alternative sources of power would eventually replace the horse-drawn fire engine as well.

In the 1880s, when this photograph was taken, the 700 block of East Franklin Street, just one block from Capitol Square downtown, was still residential. The Stewart-Lee House, second from left, was just one among many Greek Revival–style dwellings that filled Richmond's urban neighborhoods. Now they are almost all gone, except a scattered few downtown and a larger collection on Church Hill, to the east.

The rebuilding of Richmond after the Civil War stimulated the growth of many construction-related businesses and supply companies. William J. Whitehurst and Harry B. Owen formed their partnership around 1881 and manufactured window sash, blinds (shutters), and doors at this plant located at the intersection of 10th and Byrd streets near the James River.

Moldavia, which stood on the western side of 5th Street between Main and Cary streets, was constructed in several phases between about 1798 and 1820. Thomas Jefferson contributed suggestions for its architectural embellishments, and one of his workmen was hired in 1805 to enlarge the house. The most noteworthy owners, who acquired it a few years after it was completed, were John and Frances Allan. Their foster son, Edgar Allan Poe, lived there briefly in 1825 and 1826, during and after a brief, inglorious tenure as a student at the University of Virginia. Moldavia was demolished about 1890.

On May 29, 1890, hundreds of former Confederate soldiers donned their uniforms and marched to the unveiling ceremony for the Lee statue. This photograph was taken on Main Street near 10th Street, as the soldiers made their way west to Eighth Street, turned north one block to Franklin Street, then west again past the Stewart-Lee House to Monument Avenue (a continuation of Franklin Street) and the statue.

Marius-Jean-Antonin Mercié, a renowned French sculptor, created the statue of Lee on Traveller, his war horse. Photographed soon after the statue was hoisted into place, this image shows white supervisors and black workers posing on the pedestal. To the right, in front, are the grandstands erected for the unveiling ceremony; to the left rear, beneath Traveller's tail, are the buildings of Richmond College (now the University of Richmond).

Richmond National Cemetery, as it is known today, was established on September 1, 1866, as the U.S. National Military Cemetery, Richmond. It is located in the East End of Richmond on Williamsburg Road. The cemetery contains the remains of more than 3,800 men who died during the Civil War, almost all of them United States soldiers but also including at least one Confederate. Most of the soldiers are unknown. The cast-iron octagonal gazebo in the background, used as a speaker's rostrum, was erected about 1890 and removed in 1952.

RICHMOND LOCO. & MACHINE WKS.
HIGH PRESSURE CYLINDER FOR THE
BATTLE SHIP TEXAS.
MARCH 15 1890

W. E. Tanner and E. H. Betts established the Richmond Locomotive and Machine Works shortly after the Civil War. Their vast factory stood at the northern end of 7th Street, and by 1890, when this picture was taken, the workers produced two hundred locomotives a year in addition to other machinery such as this cylinder for a battleship. The factory closed around 1930.

In the 1880s and 1890s, there arose a number of "streetcar suburbs" around Richmond, including Barton Heights, shown here in the 1890s. Located just north of downtown, Barton Heights was popular with city workers for the short commute.

The Richmond Times building stood on the southeastern corner of 10th and Bank streets just below Capitol Square, and is shown here about 1893. The newspaper had been established in 1886; it merged with the *Dispatch* in 1902 to become the *Richmond Times-Dispatch,* still Richmond's principal newspaper. Eventually this building was demolished to expand the old customs house, visible on the right.

The first port of Richmond, known as Rocketts Landing, was located just below the "falls" or boulder-filled rapids of the James River. It was the highest upstream point to which oceangoing vessels could sail. Today that point is even farther downstream, because of the deeper draft of large ships. This image was taken near the old port about 1895.

Luther H. Jenkins and Elbert C. Walthall owned this bookbinding, printing, and blank-book manufacturing company, shown here about 1895. It was located at 8-12 North 12th Street.

Constructed as Park Place Methodist Episcopal Church in 1886, this spectacular Victorian Gothic structure stood opposite Monroe Park on Franklin Street until it was destroyed by arson in 1966. The church's name was changed to Pace Memorial Methodist Church in 1921 to honor benefactor James B. Pace, who donated the land on which the church was built.

Before the Civil War, Richmond was a leading producer of plug tobacco for chewing, and cigars and pipe tobacco were manufactured here as well. Cigarettes did not become popular until after the war, when Lewis Ginter, a New York–born capitalist and tobacco magnate who had come to Richmond in 1842, and his partner John F. Allen, marketed them in attractive packaging in the mid 1870s. Cigarette smoking increased rapidly, and a wide array of brands and varieties—such as My Sweetheart Cigarettes, manufactured in Lynchburg and advertised in this Main Street image—found their customers.

On June 26, 1896, the Richmond Howitzers fired a salute for the cornerstone-laying ceremonies in Monroe Park to erect a monument to Confederate President Jefferson Davis, who had died on December 11, 1889. After several competitions for a design acceptable to the United Daughters of the Confederacy, and despite the Monroe Park ceremony, the Davis monument ultimately was erected in 1907 on Monument Avenue four blocks west of the Lee monument, shown here looming in the background.

Philip K. White constructed the two-story White-Taylor House at 2717 East Grace Street, on Church Hill in Richmond's near East End, about 1839. He sold it about twenty years later to George W. Taylor, who added the third story. When White advertised the house in 1859, he mentioned its solid mahogany doors and marble mantels. For an urban dwelling, the house had several interesting outbuildings, including a dairy and two "cow houses." Today, the house is one of several antebellum architectural masterpieces on Church Hill.

St. John's Episcopal Church, on Church Hill in the eastern end of Richmond, is shown here about 1891, with children posing among the tombstones in the churchyard. It originated as the simple frame Henrico Parish church (left) in 1740, then was enlarged in 1772 with a north addition (right) that rendered the building T-shaped. The bell tower was added later. Here, on March 20, 1775, the second revolutionary convention met, and here Patrick Henry delivered the oration known as the "Liberty or Death" speech. Echoes of Henry's words continue—quite literally—to reverberate at the church, since the speech is reenacted there each March. St. John's is a National Historic Landmark.

Looking west on Main Street from about 17th Street, before the start of the twentieth century, this view shows the old market building on the right. Today the streetcar rails are gone, but a market survives and the area has enjoyed a resurgence of shops and restaurants.

This park, developed by tobacco magnate Lewis Ginter and called the Lakeside Wheel Club, was part of the neighborhood he created in the 1890s north of Richmond known as Ginter Park. Many of the houses built there then are still in high demand. The park itself is now known as the Lewis Ginter Botanical Garden.

The Virginia governor's mansion had lost some of its architectural embellishments by the time this photograph was made about 1897, especially the ornamental swags in recessed panels between the first-story and second-story windows that were part of the original design. The stork fountain was a late-nineteenth-century addition. A large-scale rehabilitation of the mansion executed in the first years of the twenty-first century removed the fountain and restored the swags.

The main building at Richmond College, Ryland Hall, was completed in 1873. The college began its life as Dunlora Academy in 1830 in Powhatan County, west of the city, then moved two years later to a location at present-day Grace and Lombardy streets— still country roads then. Chartered as Richmond College in 1840, the institution moved to its present location in the western reaches of the city as the University of Richmond in 1914.

Richmond's Reservoir Park, shown here about 1897, is now known as Byrd Park. Today a covered reservoir and three small lakes—Boat, Swan, and Shields—lie within the park, which is especially popular on summer weekends.

Into The New Century

(1900–1939)

The *Planet*, first located at 814 East Broad Street and by 1899 at 311 North 4th Street (where this picture was taken), was Richmond's pioneering black newspaper. John R. Mitchell, Jr., served as its editor from 1884 until his death in 1929. Under his leadership, the *Planet* became one of the most important African-American newspapers in the nation, crusading for civil rights and against lynching and other forms of oppression.

Richmond's elite, like the country squires of old, enjoyed riding to hounds. Many of them maintained rural estates and joined fox-hunting clubs such as the one pictured here: Deep Run Hunt of Goochland County, located west of the city.

The Swan Tavern, shown here about 1903, stood between 8th and 9th streets on the north side of Broad Street, near the Richmond, Fredericksburg, and Potomac Railroad depot. The tavern served as a hospital during the Civil War. It was torn down in 1908.

The T. W. Wood Seed Company was located in these quarters at 12 South 14th Street. Billing itself as "the Largest Seed House in the South," the company sold its seeds in spectacularly colored packets and advertised them in equally brilliant catalogs beginning about 1881. The Charles C. Hart Seed Company of Connecticut acquired T. W. Wood in 1962.

Most of Richmond's fairs were held outside the city or on its edges, but occasionally small street festivals—some as part of a business promotion—could be found downtown. This one, featuring a small Ferris wheel, probably took place around the start of the twentieth century, when Craig Art Company, located at 115 East Broad Street, sold artists' materials, pictures, and photographers' supplies.

Constructed in 1907 as the Lubin Theatre, this small but ornate building was soon renamed the Regent Theatre. It stood at 808 East Broad Street downtown and advertised "High Class Photo Plays."

The Trigg Shipbuilding Company operated in Richmond briefly around the turn of the twentieth century. Founded in 1898 by William R. Trigg, a principal in the Richmond Locomotive and Machine Works, the shipyard launched the first torpedo boat built in the South the next year, with President William McKinley officiating at the ceremonies. A few years and several cost overruns later, however, Trigg Shipbuilding went into receivership and then closed down about 1903.

Now called Old City Hall, this National Historic Landmark stands on the site of the Robert Mills city hall that was demolished in 1870, on the block between Broad, Capitol, 10th, and 11th streets. Detroit architect Elijah E. Myers designed this "new" city hall in the High Victorian Gothic style, including the spectacular interior court with Gothic arcades and flights of stairs, all in cast iron. Completed in 1894 at a cost five times the original estimate, the granite structure now houses commercial offices.

In the "olden days," as this image from about 1910 attests, a declining store did not close down with a modest "going-out-of-business sale." Instead, it admitted to being a "gigantic failure," in capital letters. To judge from the large crowd of women awaiting entry, truth-in-advertising worked, but too late. The Faulkner and Warriner Company, located at 21 East Broad Street, sold dry goods, notions, and ladies' wear.

Lewis W. Hines, investigative photographer for the National Child Labor Committee (NCLC), took this picture of two newsboys in downtown Richmond in June 1911. He identified them as "Richard Green, (with hat), 5 year old newsie, [and] Willie, who said he was 8 (Compare them). Many of these little newsboys here." Willie subsequently admitted he was only seven, and then confessed to being six. The NCLC, a private nonprofit organization founded in 1904, is still active, "promoting the rights, awareness, dignity, well-being and education of children and youth as they relate to work and working."

Turn-of-the-century Richmonders embraced the new moving pictures, but they also enjoyed vaudeville entertainment, and a large number of theaters once stood downtown. This photograph, taken in 1905, shows the north side of Broad Street at 8th Street. The Old Colonial Theater is on the left; the Bijou is on the right. In 1921, the buildings with painted-on advertisements were razed and the New Colonial Theater was erected on the site.

President Theodore Roosevelt became the nation's youngest chief executive at age forty-two on the death of President William McKinley in 1901, under whom Roosevelt served as vice president. Less than a year after winning election on his own, Roosevelt visited Richmond on October 18, 1905. The Virginia Passenger and Power Company building downtown was decorated for the occasion.

A large number of military cadets and militia units marched in the parade honoring Roosevelt. They included the cadets from Virginia Military Institute and present-day Virginia Polytechnic Institute and State University, the 70th Regiment, the Richmond Light Infantry Blues, and the Richmond Howitzers. In this image some of the troops are shown passing the decorated Virginia Building at the corner of Main and 5th streets. The office building, constructed in 1901, still stands.

Virginia Union University, a historically African American institution of higher education, is located on North Lombardy Street, north of the old downtown. The university traces its lineage to the Richmond Theological School for Freedmen, founded in 1865 and located at first in Lumpkin's Jail, a former slave pen. On February 11, 1899, the cornerstone of Kingsley Hall (center) was laid. Buffalo, New York, architect John Coxhead designed this and eight other granite buildings in the Romanesque Revival style. Six remain standing today.

Established in 1823 in the Virginia state capitol, the Virginia state library moved in 1895 into the new building shown here, which also housed the offices of the state treasurer, the auditor of public accounts, and the adjutant general, among other state agencies. An addition like the one on the north end was constructed on the south end in 1908. The governor's mansion is visible at left.

The Virginia Historical Society was established in 1831, with Chief Justice John Marshall, a Richmond resident, as its first president. The society had no permanent home until 1893, when it occupied the Stewart-Lee House at 707 East Franklin Street. Within a month of moving in, it had published the first issue of its now highly respected journal, the *Virginia Magazine of History and Biography.* In 1933, to protect its valuable and growing collection of books and artifacts, the society constructed a fireproof annex in back of the house. The society moved to its present location in Battle Abbey on Boulevard in 1946.

Richmond long had two downtown commercial centers, one on Broad Street and the other a few blocks south on Main Street. This photograph, taken on East Main Street from about 15th Street looking west, shows establishments ranging from drugstores to farm equipment salesrooms.

After a flood of the James River around 1900, clean-up is under way at the John B. Canepa and Joseph A. Baccigalupo grocery store and saloon at 1615 East Franklin Street, with the Giuseppe Massei Saloon next door at 1613. Richmond, which had a total population of 85,050 that year, had 217 saloons. Despite ongoing efforts to ban the sale of alcoholic beverages in Virginia, it was not until November 1916 that statewide prohibition went into effect, and saloonkeepers like these had to turn their attention strictly to groceries.

The Jefferson Davis Monument was unveiled in a ceremony held on June 3, 1907, the ninety-ninth anniversary of his birth. Davis had served as U.S. secretary of war and as a U.S. senator from Mississippi during the antebellum years, and before the Civil War, as a national figure he was better known than Abraham Lincoln. It is fair to say that Davis's prickly personality kept him from being as beloved by Southerners during his lifetime as Lee was during his, but in his later years, Davis became the focus of much Confederate nostalgia. He died in New Orleans on December 11, 1889, and was buried in Hollywood Cemetery.

The central building in this composition is Ryland Hall, the main building of the University of Richmond. Taken about 1909, the photograph shows the university at its late-nineteenth-century location, bounded by Broad, Ryland, Lombardy, and Franklin streets. Although Ryland Hall, which had a central tower crowned with a French Second Empire roof, appears to be a unified structure, in fact it was constructed in at least three phases between 1855 and 1876. One of the wings burned in 1910, when plans were already afoot to move the institution to its present location in Westhampton, west of the urban center. Ryland Hall was demolished about 1920.

For many years, farm produce was brought into the city in horse-drawn carts to be sold at street markets like this one on 6th and Marshall streets. This image was captured in 1908. Today's street vendors of locally grown produce more typically operate from small trucks and stands in the suburbs.

New York architect Joseph H. McGuire designed the Cathedral of the Sacred Heart, which faces Monroe Park and downtown Richmond at the edge of the city's residential Fan District. Thomas Fortune Ryan, a native Virginian and Roman Catholic financier and philanthropist, funded the cathedral, which was begun in 1903 and completed in 1906. Its architectural style is Renaissance Revival, and the interior is richly decorated with Renaissance-style embellishments.

The Male Orphan Asylum was established late in the 1840s and stood for many years on the corner of Baker and St. James streets in what was then the northern part of Richmond. It was the forerunner of the Virginia Home for Boys, which still operates on West Broad Street.

This triple-decker railroad crossing, located in Shockoe Bottom near the James River at 17th and Dock streets, is reputed to be the only such crossing in America. Over the years, several trains have posed there for photographers, including these in 1911. From top to bottom, the rail lines represented are the Chesapeake and Ohio, the Seaboard, and the Southern.

Goddin's Tavern, located on Brook Road north of Richmond, as seen about the turn of the century. The image depicts an eighteenth-century inn almost as it appeared during its heyday. Constructed late in the 1700s and first known as Baker's Tavern for owner Martin Baker, the building stood on what was at the time the main road leading into Richmond from the north. In 1835, John Goddin acquired the inn, and he operated it for about 20 years. The construction of large hotels in Richmond, as well as the Civil War, helped bring about its decline. In its last years, the inn served as a saloon. It was demolished in 1912.

When President William Howard Taft visited Richmond on November 11, 1909, he was escorted from Main Street Station to the governor's mansion, where he was given breakfast. He next addressed the Virginia Press Association in the House of Delegates, and then he met with Richmond's African American leaders in the State Corporation Commission room in the capitol. Standing on the steps in front of the capitol's portico, the group included Giles B. Jackson (back row, second from left), a former slave who became an attorney after the war and was the first black to practice before the Virginia supreme court of appeals, as well as John B. Mitchell, Jr., crusading editor of the *Richmond Planet* (front row, fifth from left).

The two young people seated in the automobile in the circular driveway in front of the governor's mansion are "Miss Cousins" and William H. Mann, Jr., son of Virginia governor William Hodges Mann (1910–1914). The eastern end of the capitol is visible on the left, and the Washington equestrian statue and the bell tower of St. Paul's Church can be seen on the right. Several early automobiles were manufactured in Richmond, but this model and its provenance are not identified.

The electric streetcars pioneered in Richmond in 1888 soon spread throughout the world and encouraged the explosive growth of "streetcar suburbs" around urban centers. Various streetcar lines linked far-flung parts of Richmond by early in the twentieth century. Here, at Broad and Seventh streets in the heart of downtown, a streetcar from Hull Street in Manchester on the south side of the James River (an independent city until annexed by Richmond in 1910), discharges commuters.

Richmond's wealthy elite belonged to exclusive men's clubs, such as the Commonwealth Club and the Westmoreland Club, around the turn of the century. For the working man, the saloon served the same purpose as a club. In the saloons men could gather after a hard day's labor, quaff some beer, discuss the topics of the day, and enjoy a convivial atmosphere. There were others, however, who were convinced—not altogether without reason—that "drink is the curse of the working classes," and who were determined to put the saloons out of business. On the occasion of their thirteenth convention, members of the Anti-Saloon League of Virginia pose on the south steps of the Virginia state capitol on January 21, 1914. With the introduction of Prohibition a short time later, their dream became a grim reality for both workingmen and saloonkeepers.

Even in urban residential areas, where streets had been paved for years, nature intruded occasionally. Working on Park Avenue in Richmond's residential Fan District in 1915, laborers cut down a massive oak growing in the street, then posed with onlookers beside the hollow stump before removing it.

This elegant building, located at the corner of 8th and Main streets, housed the Morris Plan Bank of Richmond (established 1922). The bank, renamed the Morris Plan Bank of Virginia in 1928, was the brainchild of Arthur J. Morris. He provided loans to individuals who could not obtain them elsewhere, on the basis of "good character" and two cosigners or collateral.

This view, probably taken in the 1920s looking west from Capitol Square, includes the familiar—the Richmond Hotel, the Washington Monument, and St. Paul's Church—as well as the new: the Virginia Electric and Power Company building on the far left. Established in 1925, the company kept its headquarters in this elaborate building with its electrical-gadget "spires." Today the spires are gone, and VEPCO (now Dominion) is headquartered elsewhere, but the old building still stands at Franklin and 7th streets.

Hard freezes seldom occur in Richmond, but when they do, those who enjoy ice skating take advantage of them. This temporarily frozen lake is located in Byrd Park.

Between the city hall on the left and the Virginia state capitol on the right, a cleared lot bounded by Broad, 11th, 12th, and Capitol streets marks the site of Ford's Hotel, also known as the Powhatan House. Constructed about 1840, the hotel stood at the epicenter of Virginia politics, just across Capitol Street from the capitol and the governor's mansion, and opposite 11th Street from Richmond's government center. The city bought the hotel in 1911 and demolished it to build a municipal courthouse. The lot remained vacant until the Virginia state library was built there in 1938–1941.

This aerial view from September 3, 1920, depicts Broad Street Station, which was completed in 1919 for the Richmond, Fredericksburg, and Potomac Railroad and the Atlantic Coast Line Railroad. Architect John Russell Pope, who designed the Jefferson Memorial and the National Gallery of Art in Washington, D.C., designed the building.

John Russell Pope's 1919 Broad Street Station, the nation's first domed central railroad station, was executed in Indiana limestone, with an impressive Tuscan colonnade. Today the building is home to the Science Museum of Virginia.

Before 1922, Chamberlayne Avenue, a main approach from the northern suburb of Ginter Park south to Richmond, ended at Duval Street. In the summer of that year, however, the avenue was extended south to Leigh Street. The extension cut diagonally across a residential block, resulting in the demolition of several dwellings and the moving of at least one.

The Hotel Richmond, located at 9th and Grace streets just west of Capitol Square, replaced the Hotel Claire in 1904. After the demolition of Ford's Hotel in 1911, it became the only hotel on Capitol Hill, and was frequented by legislators and those doing business with the General Assembly because of its proximity to the square. The photograph here shows the hotel about 1924. Today, it houses state offices and is called the Ninth Street Office Building.

Ferruccio Legnaioli sculptured the statue of Christopher Columbus that stands at the northern end of Byrd Park gazing up Boulevard. It was dedicated on December 9, 1927, the first monument to Columbus erected in the South. The flappers shown here—Eleanora T. Corrieri and Anna Guarina—wrapped themselves in the flags used during the unveiling ceremony and then posed on the statue.

Richmond's East End, as well as the other areas of the city, received road improvements in the 1920s. The men shown here are working on Government Road at National Street, looking toward the U.S. National Cemetery on Williamsburg Road, sometime in 1927.

Taken in May 1927, this image of the south side of Broad Street looking west from 8th Street shows the Miller and Rhoads department store on the left. Together with Thalhimer's department store, located one block east on the corner of 7th Street, Miller and Rhoads was the retail anchor of Broad Street.

Photographed at Marshall and Adams streets in Jackson Ward in 1929, this street-repair crew is bringing progress to one of Richmond's historic African-American neighborhoods.

Christmas shoppers crowd the sidewalks at 5th and Broad streets near McCrory's late in the 1920s. The Great Depression had not yet struck, and newspapers reported record-breaking sales for the holiday season. Retail merchants, wrote a reporter, "have employed hundreds of extra clerks to take care of the pre-holiday demand."

The Shockoe Bottom area of Richmond is the oldest part of the city and has been home to a mixture of industrial and residential buildings since the 1700s. This August 1929 view shows East Cary Street at South 17th Street looking west. Industrial buildings, like Brown-Mooney Supply Company at 1701 East Cary Street to the left, lined both sides of the street and the elevated Richmond, Fredericksburg, and Potomac Railroad track crossed the area a block from Main Street Station. Both gasoline-powered and horse-drawn vehicles can be seen on the street. All of the buildings shown here are now gone, obliterated by Interstate 95, and concrete piers have replaced the trestle's iron supports.

This aerial view of Battle Abbey, today the home of the Virginia Historical Society, was captured in the 1920s. In 1912, the Confederate Memorial Association laid the cornerstone for the Confederate Memorial Institute, usually known as "Battle Abbey," as a shrine to the Confederate war dead and as a repository for the Lost Cause records. The impetus for the building came from Virginia Civil War veteran Charles Broadway Rouss, who had made his fortune in New York. Rouss contributed $100,000, half of the amount required to erect the building. Veterans' camps, schoolchildren, and ladies' organizations throughout the South contributed the rest in small amounts.

On November 11, 1929, Frederick W. Sievers's statue of Commodore Matthew Fontaine Maury, "the Pathfinder of the Seas," was unveiled on Richmond's Monument Avenue by two of the commodore's great-grandchildren, Mary Maury Fitzgerald and Matthew Fontaine Maury Osborne. Maury became superintendent of the U.S. Navy Department's Depot of Charts and Instruments (later the Naval Observatory) in 1842 and published the first textbook of modern oceanography, *The Physical Geography of the Sea* (1855). On the basis of his work, Maury is credited with founding the science of oceanography. His system for collecting and using oceanographic data revolutionized the navigation of the seas.

The popularity of vegetable markets such as the 6th Street Market remained high in the 1930s, when this photograph was taken. Automobiles now crowded the street instead of horses and carts.

Over the centuries, Virginia's governors have been inaugurated at various locations in Capitol Square. For many years, the ceremonies took place under the south portico, as in the case of Governor John Garland Pollard's inauguration on January 15, 1930. More recently, however, a temporary dais and grandstands have been erected on the north side of the capitol to accommodate the large crowds that now attend.

The painted sign advertising the Greek-Italian Importing Company in this picture of 6th Street is a reminder that Richmond was long a city of immigrants. Before the Civil War, its percentage of foreign-born residents was unusually high for a Southern city. Until late in the twentieth century, when the city became home to a relatively large number of ethnic restaurants, many Richmonders looked forward to the annual International Food Festival. Large numbers of ethnic-food booths, staffed by immigrants from every part of the world who had settled in Richmond, always attracted huge and appreciative crowds.

Richmond has long been home to a number of open-air markets. This one is located at 6th Street and was photographed by the Federal Security Administration's W. Lincoln Highton late in the 1930s. The picture was used to illustrate Virginia's volume, *Virginia: A Guide to the Old Dominion*, in the American Guide Series, which was sponsored by the Work Projects Administration. The volume was compiled by workers of the Virginia Writers' Program and published in 1940.

Pratt's Castle, from which the Civil War panoramas at the beginning of this book were photographed, had undergone some alterations by the 1930s, when this image was captured, but its outlines were unchanged. The castle stood on Gamble's Hill until 1956, when it was demolished for a corporate headquarters amid a national protest.

The Thalhimer's department store at 601 East Broad Street was one of Richmond's best-loved shopping emporiums before it closed in 1992. Thalhimer's originated in 1842 when William Thalhimer, a German immigrant, opened a dry-goods store on North 17th Street between Main and Franklin streets and five years later moved it to 18th and Main. After the Civil War, Thalhimer reopened his business on Broad Street, and in 1877 he turned it over to his sons, who renamed it Thalhimer Brothers. By 1890 the brothers had two dry-goods stores at 501 and at 609 East Broad Street. Twenty-five years later, a grandson of the founder bought out his father and an uncle and expanded the department store aspects of the business. In 1922 the store was incorporated and relocated into a five-story building on Broad Street between 6th and 7th streets. This view of the 6th Street side of the store shows the section designed with art deco elements by the New York architectural firm of Tausig and Fleich in 1939.

The second of Richmond's beloved major department stores was Miller and Rhoads. Begun in 1885 by Linton Miller, Webster Rhoads, and Simon Gerhart at 117 East Broad Street, the dry-goods store was called Miller, Rhoads, and Gerhart and advertised that it had "One Price for All." In 1888, it moved to 500-511 East Broad Street, and two years later, in 1890, Gerhart opened a store in Lynchburg, leaving the Richmond store as Miller and Rhoads. By 1909, the store had grown to encompass more than half a block on Broad Street. Miller and Rhoads offered every service possible for the customer's convenience, including a service desk with telephones and delivery of the customer's packages even if purchased at another store. It closed in 1990.

Between 1918 and 1924 construction on the Grace Street side of Miller and Rhoads enlarged the store to cover a city block between Broad and Grace and 5th and 6th streets. The store also grew to five stories with the facade seen in this 1930s photograph and billed itself as "the Shopping Center." Miller and Rhoads was so successful that the owners air-conditioned it in 1935 and installed escalators. Its famous Tea Room, the first in Virginia, featured fashion shows, the organ music of Eddie Weaver, and signature menu items like the Missouri Club sandwich, Brunswick stew, and chocolate silk pie. Miller and Rhoads is most famous, however, for having the "real" Santa Claus, who came to the store just before the beginning of World War II.

This picture of 6th Street Market, taken late in the 1930s by W. Lincoln Highton, was used as an illustration in *Virginia: A Guide to the Old Dominion,* published under the auspices of the Work Projects Administration. Markow Florists, whose sign is visible at left, began as a peddler's street cart in the market in 1922. It moved into 304 North 6th Street soon thereafter, and remained there until 1978, when it moved again to a store on East Broad Street. This Richmond institution sold its assets to Strange's Florist in 2006 and ceased operations.

According to tradition, the Richmond Light Infantry Blues were established on May 10, 1793, although the same date in 1789 is sometimes suggested. It was one of several local militia units raised for local protection in the years following the Revolutionary War, when most Americans disliked the idea of a standing army. The Blues were called into service at various times, including during the Civil War and later in World War II as part of the 29th Infantry Division. The unit was disbanded in 1968. Its armory still stands at 6th and Marshall streets. In this photograph the Blues march in Richmond to celebrate their 140th anniversary.

In 1893, railroad magnate and philanthropist Major James H. Dooley and his wife, Sallie May Dooley, built a late-Victorian mansion on farmland purchased on the James River west of downtown Richmond. When completed, Maymont House boasted the latest modern conveniences: electric lighting, an elevator, three full bathrooms, and central heat. At the beginning of the 1900s, the Dooleys commissioned the Richmond firm of Noland and Baskervill to design an Italian garden at Maymont. Modeling the garden on elements of the classical style devised in the fifteenth and sixteenth centuries in Italy, the firm incorporated characteristic features including fountains, geometrically shaped beds, sculpture, and a long pergola situated along the garden's northern edge. In keeping with the classical ideal, the garden was laid out in several levels and situated on a south-facing slope overlooking the water. Completed in 1910, the garden, seen here in the 1930s, has become the scene of many Richmond weddings following Maymont's transition to a public park after the death of Mrs. Dooley in 1925.

The Forty-Second Confederate Reunion took place in Richmond, June 21-24, 1932. Although no one realized it then, it would be the last time the old soldiers would gather for a large reunion. At 11:30 on the morning of June 24, the grand review got under way, as the grand marshal, Virginia's lieutenant governor, and other officials left Capitol Square, drove west on Grace Street to 5th Street, turned south, then turned west again on Franklin Street. The Sons of Confederate Veterans joined the procession at the John Marshall Hotel, the Confederated Southern Memorial Association members joined at the Jefferson Hotel, and finally the United Confederate Veterans fell in at the R. E. Lee Camp Confederate Soldiers' Home. The parade then made its way past the statues of Stuart, Lee, Davis, and Jackson on Monument Avenue as vast crowds cheered.

It was not all meetings, lectures, and parades at the 1932 Confederate Reunion in Richmond. Dinners, teas, and balls were given, and entertainment venues were located at various points throughout the city. The veterans and sightseers beheld a large and varied number of performers, including a one-man band, a human saxophone ("A Jazz Wonder"), old-time fiddlers, Hack and Sack ("In Person"), a madrigal quartet, and several concert bands. In this photograph, perhaps taken at the Soldiers' Home, some of the old veterans dance to favorite tunes performed by a banjo and fiddle band.

James N. O'Neil, Sr., started the O.K. Foundry—"A Family Owned American Foundry Since 1912"—to supply the local railroad, tobacco, and agricultural industries with made-to-order cast iron. By 1948, the business had outgrown its original barnlike building and another location at 14 East 7th Street, thus moving into its current location at 1005 Commerce Road. It is still family owned and produces gray and ductile iron for engineering uses and ornamental iron castings.

The Richmond home of Chief Justice John Marshall, pictured here late in the 1930s, is a National Historic Landmark. He constructed the Georgian-style dwelling in 1790 and lived there for the next 45 years. Here he wrote many of the decisions that established the independence of the judiciary in the young Republic. Threatened with demolition in 1907, the house was rescued by the Association for the Preservation of Virginia Antiquities, later restored, and opened as a house museum. John Marshall High School, built to the rear of the house about 1909, has since been demolished.

The only surviving colonial house in Richmond, the Ege House became the Poe Museum in 1922. This photograph of the house was taken in 1939 and placed in one of the albums of Virginia photographs that graced the Virginia Room in the Court of States at the 1939 New York World's Fair. The Poe Museum is home to the world's finest collection of Edgar Allan Poe manuscripts, letters, first editions, memorabilia, and personal belongings. The Old Stone House is only blocks away from the sites of Poe's first Richmond home and his first place of employment, the Southern Literary Messenger.

In 1932, as Richmonders faced an average 10 percent reduction in take-home pay caused by the Depression, some good news arrived with the decision of the federal Reconstruction Finance Corporation to fund a new bridge across the James River at Oregon Hill. Begun in 1933, the new Robert E. Lee Bridge was completed in 1934 and cost $1.13 million, $822,000 of which was spent on the bridge itself and the rest on the approaches.

The workers in this picture and the one preceding are on the north bank of the river, preparing the hillside at Oregon Hill on the western side for the construction of the bridge and working with wheelbarrows on the eastern side of the bridge area. At first tolls were levied to cross the new bridge, but they were finally ended in 1946.

This view of the Egyptian Building covered in ivy was taken in 1939 and is included in one of the albums of Virginia photographs that graced the Virginia Room in the Court of States at the 1939 New York World's Fair. The Egyptian Building is considered America's masterpiece of Egyptian Revival–style architecture. Thomas S. Stewart, of Philadelphia, designed it in the 1840s, and it was completed in 1846. It originally housed Hampden-Sydney College's medical department, which had moved to Richmond in 1837. Today the building is the architectural symbol of Virginia Commonwealth University School of Medicine, the successor to the early medical school. The style of the building, a National Historic Landmark, represents Egypt's ancient medical tradition, with the granite piers in the shape of obelisks.

Richmond once had several early nineteenth-century houses with demioctagonal bays such as the Hancock-Wirt-Caskie House at 2 North 5th Street; now it is the only one left. The high-quality arcaded galleries, brickwork, and interior woodwork make it especially distinctive. Michael Hancock constructed the dwelling in 1809, and attorney William Wirt purchased it in 1816. It was while living here that Wirt completed his biography of Patrick Henry, which included Henry's "Liberty or Death" speech. Henry, as was his custom, had spoken without notes, so Wirt reconstructed the speech by corresponding with the surviving members of the revolutionary convention who had been present when it was delivered, including Thomas Jefferson. The current owner of the house has for years been undertaking a meticulous, museum-quality restoration. This photograph was taken in 1936.

Seen here in 1940, 8th Street looking north from Canal Street shows the back of the Richmond Times-Dispatch printing plant and a side view of the Noland Company, purveyors of wholesale plumbing and heating supplies. In the 1920s, the Richmond Times-Dispatch moved its printing plant to 107–119 South 7th Street, where the company installed a new three-unit Hoe press that could print 40,000 copies per hour. The owners also brought in a new color press, which was used to print the comics for about 30 other newspapers across the South. In 1938, the Times-Dispatch purchased another press, an "eight-unit Hoe super-production unit-type newspaper printing press with two super-production double former folders." It stood three stories tall, weighed 304 tons, and used the "hot-type" system of molten lead to form the newspaper copy. The paper reported to its readers that with the new press "your *Times-Dispatch* now comes fresh and crisply printed every morning from a press as modern as any in the newspaper world"—"the latest juggernaut of the printed word."

The Modern City

(1940–1969)

This overview of the capitol was taken from the new Medical College of Virginia building about 1942. In the distance can be seen some of the city's financial district and the James River. The foreground shows the southeastern corner of the newly opened Virginia State Library and the governor's mansion. Beyond the governor's mansion stands the old state library building, called thereafter the Finance Building, and the State Office Building tower.

The Robert E. Lee Bridge, photographed here in 1947, was constructed in 1933–1934 across the James River at Belle Isle. It connected Belvidere on the north side of the river with Cowardin Avenue on the south side. The bridge was closed and demolished when a new bridge was completed in 1988.

Relocated to 300 South 6th Street in 1910, Binswanger and Company, the triangular building seen here in a 1940 photograph (center), was started by Samuel Binswanger in 1872 as a paint supply store on Broad Street. Nine years later, the firm branched out into building supplies, including paints, oils, window sash, doors, and blinds. By 1910, Binswanger's sons had turned to glass products and services, and by the beginning of World War II had expanded the business into the Carolinas, Tennessee, and Texas. Today the company supplies residential, commercial, and automotive replacement glass, has more than 150 locations in 22 states, and has become the largest full-service glass retailer in the United States.

The Finance Building, located next to the Executive Mansion, as seen about 1940. Constructed between 1892 and 1894, the Finance Building was built to house the state's reference library and archives, which had previously been located in the capitol. The building also held the offices of the auditor of public accounts, the state treasurer, and several other governmental departments. Hours of operation for the new state library in the early days were 9 A.M. to 3 P.M. The City of Richmond provided a "night clerk" to offer access to the public from 7 P.M. to midnight. In addition to a large reading room and reference areas, the new library also displayed maps, portraits, and statuary from its collections. After the state library moved to its new art deco building across Governor Street from Capitol Square in December 1940, the old library building became the Finance Building to reflect its new function.

There actually was a time, at least according to Richmond urban legend, when visitors to Capitol Square were forbidden to walk or sit on the grass. That time had passed by the 1940s, when these women sat on the lawn in the summer to enjoy lunch. As the principal green space in the heart of downtown Richmond, Capitol Square continues to be utilized for outdoor lunching and sunbathing.

This photograph of the Triple Crossing was taken in 1949. The contrast between the streamlkined seaboard engine and the old-fashioned Chesapeake & Ohio locomotive is striking. This photograph would be difficult to duplicate today because of the construction of the nearby flood wall.

On November 25, 1949, Richmond's electric streetcar system, the first in the nation, came to a close. Automobiles and buses had supplanted the antiquated system. Officials bid good-bye to the streetcars as the trolleys made their last run in the city. Today one of the trolley cars can still be seen at the Virginia Historical Society's long-term exhibition, "The Story of Virginia: An American Experience."

This view of Main and 8th streets, with a Republican banner hanging across Main Street, was captured in 1952. For the second time in the 1900s, Richmond left the Democratic fold that year and voted for Dwight D. Eisenhower for president, giving him 29,300 votes to the Democrat Adlai Stevenson's 19,233. On September 26, Eisenhower campaigned in Richmond, cheered by 30,000 people along the route as his motorcade drove from Broad Street Station to the capitol, where he was greeted by another 20,000 Richmonders chanting, "We want Ike!"

Looking south toward Main Street from Broad Street in the 1960s, this image shows the tracks entering the train shed of Main Street Station. The recently constructed Interstate 95 curves around the station.

In September 1967, the Richmond Braves, the Atlanta Braves' Triple-A baseball team, were in the hunt for the first International League pennant in the team's history. Seen here at the city's Parker Field on September 3, the crowds in the stands cheered the players as they battled the Toledo Mud Hens in a three-to-one loss. Two days later, however, Richmond finally won its first International Pennant by beating the Rochester Red Wings two-to-nothing in a special playoff after the two teams were tied at the end of the regular season.

Today's Virginia Commonwealth University was founded in 1917 as the Richmond School of Social Work and Public Health and was located in the Richmond Juvenile Court building on Capitol Street. It became the Richmond Division of the College of William and Mary in 1925 and moved to its present location near Monroe Park that year. The school's name was changed to Richmond Professional Institute in 1939. In 1962, the Institute separated from William and Mary and became independent. Six years later, it merged with the Medical College of Virginia to form Commonwealth University. This photograph, taken in 1966, shows Richmond Professional Institute's urban environment.

The north side of downtown Broad Street (right) has changed dramatically since this picture was taken in 1967 looking west from the top of the Medical College of Virginia hospital building. Few of the buildings, from the Flame Sandwich Shop on to the middle distance, remain standing. New City Hall and the new Library of Virginia, built over the next three decades, are perhaps the most significant additions to the cityscape.

NOTES ON THE PHOTOGRAPHS

These notes, listed by page number, attempt to include all aspects known of the photographs. Each of the photographs is identified by the page number, a title or description, photographer and collection, archive, and call or box number when applicable. Although every attempt was made to collect all data, in some cases complete data may have been unavailable due to the age and condition of some of the photographs and records.

II   BELL TOWER   7
Library of Virginia
001015_03

VI   PRATT'S CASTLE   8
Library of Virginia
00407u

X   TELEGRAPH
CONSTRUCTION
WAGON TRAIN   9
Library of Virginia
070377_002

2   U.S. SANITARY
COMMISSION   10
Library of Virginia
070377_003

3   CONTRABAND
CAMP   11
Library of Virginia
070377_004

4   CASTLE THUNDER
Library of Virginia   12
070377_005

5   BRIDGE PIERS
Library of Virginia
070377_005   13

6   TREDEGAR IRON
WORKS
Linbrary of
Congress
cwpb 02711

RUINED   14
LOCOMOTIVE
Library of Congress
cwpb 02704

RUINS OF FLOUR   15
MILLS
Library of Virginia
070377_007
    16
RUINS OF CARY
STREET
Library of Virginia
070377_008   17

U.S. CUSTOMS
HOUSE
Library of Virginia   18
070377_009

VIRGINIA STATE
CAPITOL   19
Library of Congress
cwpb 02515

GOVERNOR'S   20
MANSION
Library of Virginia
070377_011
    21
STATUE OF HENRY
CLAY
Library of Virginia
021641_01

BROCKENBROUGH   22
HOUSE
Library of Virginia
070377_044

MORSON'S ROW
Library of Congress   23
cwpb 00450

CUSTOMS HOUSE
Library of Congress
cwpb 02889
    24
OLD STONE HOUSE
Library of Virginia
070377_016
    26
SPOTSWOOD HOTEL
Library of Congress
cwpb 00451

MONROE TOMB   27
Library of Congress
cwpb 02923

JAMES RIVER   28
Library of Congress
cwpb 02677

MONUMENTAL
CHURCH   29
Library of Virginia
070377_0054

CONFEDERATE   30
SOLDIERS
MONUMENT
Library of Virginia
070377_015
    31
JAMES RIVER
SWELL
Library of Virginia
070179_The
Bottom 187   32

RICHMOND THEATRE
Library of Virginia
070377_031   33

CIVIL
RECONCILIATION
Library of Virginia
060551_01   34

RICHMOND SKYLINE
Library of Virginia
070377_150   35

HORSE-DRAWN
CARS
Library of Virginia
070377_080
    36
PASSENGER
STREETCAR
Library of Virginia
070377_021

EAST FRANKLIN
STREET
Library of Virginia
070377_026

MANUFACTURING
PLANTS
Library of Virginia
000782_02

MOLDAVIA
Library of Virginia
002503_01a

CONFEDERATE
SOLDIERS
Library of Virginia
070377_034

LEE ON TRAVELLER
Library of Virginia
992007_07

RICHMOND
NATIONAL
CEMETERY
Library of Virginia
070377_027

RICHMOND
LOCOMOTIVE
Library of Virginia
070377_032

37   STREETCAR SUBURB
Library of Virginia
070377_033

38 **RICHMOND TIMES**
Library of Virginia
070377_035

39 **ROCKETTS LANDING**
Library of Virginia
070377_038

40 **JENKINS AND WALTHALL**
Library of Virginia
070377_039

41 **PARK PLACE METHODIST**
Library of Virginia
070377_040

42 **SWEETHEART CIGARETTES**
Library of Virginia
070377_046

43 **MONROE PARK**
Library of Virginia
070377_152

44 **WHITE TAYLOR HOUSE**
Library of Virginia
070377_047

45 **ST. JOHN'S EPISCOPAL**
Library of Virginia
070377_079

46 **MAIN STREET**
Library of Virginia
070377_04969

47 **LAKESIDE WHEEL CLUB**
Library of Virginia
070377_051

48 **GOVERNOR'S MANSION**
Library of Virginia
040881_01

49 **RYLAND HALL**
Library of Virginia
070377_052

50 **RESERVOIR PARK**
Library of Virginia
070377_053

52 **THE PLANET**
Library of Congress
cph 3c18032

53 **DEEP RUN HUNT**
Library of Virginia
070377_058

54 **SWAN TAVERN**
Library of Virginia
070377_059

55 **WOOD SEED COMPANY**
Library of Virginia
070377_060

56 **STREET FESTIVAL**
Library of Virginia
070377_062

57 **LUBIN THEATRE**
Library of Virginia
070377_024

58 **TRIGG SHIPBUILDING**
Library of Virginia
070377_063

59 **OLD CITY HALL**
Library of Virginia
070377_153

60 **FAULKNER AND WARRINER**
Library of Virginia
070377_154

61 **NEWSBOYS**
Library of Congress
03726u

62 **OLD COLONIAL THEATRE**
Library of Virginia
070377_087

63 **ROOSEVELT CELEBRATION**
Library of Virginia
070377_06595

64 **ROOSEVELT PARADE**
Library of Virginia
070377_149

65 **UNION UNIVERSITY**
Library of Congress
PAN US GEOG-
Virginia no. 38

66 **VIRGINIA STATE LIBRARY**
Library of Virginia
010792_07

67 **STUART LEE HOUSE**
Library of Virginia
070377_081

68 **EAST MAIN STREET**
Library of Virginia
070377_071

69 **GROCERY STORE**
Library of Virginia
070377_108

70 **JEFFERSON DAVIS MONUMENT**
Library of Virginia
070377_084

71 **RYLAND HALL**
Library of Congress
PAN US GEOG-
Virginia no.
37106

72 **MARSHALL STREET**
Library of Virginia
070377_074

73 **CATHEDRAL OF THE SACRED HEART**
Library of Virginia
070377_075

74 **MALE ORPHAN ASYLUM**
Library of Virginia
070377_072

75 **SHOCKOE BOTTOM**
Library of Virginia
990856_06

76 **GODDIN'S TAVERN**
Library of Virginia
070377_076

77 **STATE CORPORATION COMMISSION**
Library of Virginia
012140_04

78 **MISS COUSINS**
Library of Virginia
03392

79 **STREET CAR**
Library of Virginia
070377_086

82 **ANTI-SALOON LEAGUE**
Library of Congress
LOT 5599 no. 5

81 **PARK AVENUE**
Library of Virginia
070377_092

82 **MORRIS PLAN BANK**
Library of Virginia
070377_042

83 **CAPITOL SQUARE**
Library of Virginia
050425_01

84 **BYRD PARK ICESKATING**
Library of Virginia
070377_089

85 **POWHATAN HOUSE**
Library of Virginia
00105_06

86 **BROAD STREET STATION**
Library of Virginia
990856_02

87 **BROAD STREET STATION**
Library of Virginia
003

88 **CHAMBERLAYNE AVE.**
Library of Virginia
070377_094

89 **HOTEL RICHMOND**
Library of Virginia
070377_095

90 **COLUMBUS STATUE**
Library of Virginia
070377_096

91 **EAST END**
Library of Virginia
070377_097

92 **BROAD STREET**
Library of Virginia
070377_101

93 **STREET REPAIR CREW**
Library of Virginia
070377_102

94 **CHRISTMAS SHOPPERS**
Library of Virginia
070377_157

95 **SHOCKOE BOTTOM AREA**
Library of Virginia
070377_103

96 **BATTLE ABBEY**
Library of Virginia
070377_110

97 **SIEVERS' STATUE**
Library of Virginia
070377_115

98 **SIXTH STREET MARKET**
Library of Virginia
98502_04

99 **CAPITOL SOUTH PORTICO**
Library of Virginia
070377_099

100 GREEK-ITALIAN IMPORTING
Library of Virginia
070377_100

101 OPEN-AIR MARKET
Library of Virginia
011925_04

102 PRATT'S CASTLE
Library of Virginia
070377_088

103 THALHIMER'S
Library of Virginia
991088-04152

104 MILLER AND RHOADS
Library of Virginia
070377_107

105 SHOPPING CENTER UPGRADE
Library of Virginia
070377_109

106 SIXTH STREET MARKET
Library of Virginia
011925_03

107 LIGHT INFANTRY BLUES
Library of Virginia
070377_090

108 MAYMONT HOUSE
Library of Virginia
070377_112

109 FORTY-SECOND CONFEDERATE UNION
Library of Virginia
003115-15

110 CONFEDERATE REUNION
Library of Virginia
070377_114

111 O.K. FOUNDRY
Library of Virginia
070267

112 MARSHALL HOME
Library of Congress
HABS VA, 44-RICH,4-2

113 POE MUSEUM
Library of Virginia
WF-07-05-004

114 OREGON HILL
Library of Virginia
070377_118

115 BRIDGE EFFORT
Library of Virginia
070377_119

116 EGYPTIAN BUILDING
Library of Virginia
WF-07-05-01

117 WIRT-CASKIE HOUSE
Library of Congress
HABS VA,44-RICH,2-1

118 EIGHTH STREET
Library of Virginia
070377_121

120 CAPITOL OVERVIEW
Library of Virginia
070377_113

121 LEE BRIDGE
Library of Virginia
070377_098

122 BINSWANGER
Library of Virginia
070377_122

123 FINANCE BUILDING
Library of Virginia
010792-05

124 CAPITOL SQUARE
Library of Virginia
070377_126

125 TRIPLE CROSSING
Library of Virginia
011925)_05

126 ELECTRIC STREETCAR
Library of Virginia
070377_136

127 MAIN STREET
Library of Virginia
070377_127

128 MAIN STREET
Library of Virginia
011925_06

129 RICHMOND BRAVES
Library of Virginia
070149-14

130 V.C.U.
Library of Virginia
070377_144

131 BROAD STREET
Library of Virginia
070377_147

Printed in the USA
CPSIA information can be obtained
at www.ICGtesting.com
JSHW061405021023
49513JS00027B/1138

9 781683 368786